50 Real

More terrifying real life encounters with ghosts and spirits

"While yet a boy I sought for ghosts, and sped
Through many a listening chamber, cave and ruin,
And starlight wood, with fearful steps pursuing
Hopes of high talk with the departed dead."

PERCY BYSSHE SHELLEY, Hymn to Intellectual Beauty

eBook version December 2012

978-1-909667-04-4 - eBook-ePub
978-1-909667-05-1 - Mobi
978-1-909667-06-8 - PDF
978-1-909667-07-5 - Paperback

Published by Hob Hill Books
www.hobhill.com

Author website
www.mjwayland.com

CONTENTS

FOREWORD

I did not expect 50 Real Ghost Stories to be the success that it has been and continues to be – I doubted whether readers would appreciate reading firsthand and very bizarre accounts of paranormal activity and not the usual edited stories that are often published.

With three decades of experience of investigating and researching paranormal activity, I am lucky in that I have many case notes and witness statements sitting in my archive. This is my last collection of witness's ghost stories and so have really pulled together a collection of the scariest, strangest and unnerving REAL experiences you will have ever read.

The book will take you on a journey through haunted houses, ghosts of the work place and even road ghosts – the type that smile at you as you hit them in your car! This book certainly isn't for the fainthearted because you have it from me – that these are REAL encounters with the unknown.

Thank you for buying my book and now I hope to scare you somewhat.

MJ Wayland
December 2012

GHOST IN THE WOODS

My experience took place next to Black Fan Road, Welwyn Garden City. The woods next to the road are alleged to be haunted.

One Friday night I was out at the pub with my friend, we had enough to drink and were a little bit tipsy but not too bad to walk home. It was around 11.30pm and we decided to go on a little walk and ended up on Black Fan Road, temptation was too much for us so we walked through the woods. There is a long path that goes through the woods, on the left side of the path is dense woodland which was very dark on this night.

We were walking in there for about ten minutes telling each other jokes until I noticed a man with a walking stick about fifty metres in front of us. I informed my friend and we sobered up quickly! The man with the walking stick was walking in and out of the trees but hard to see so we walked faster to see what was happening. We looked around for at least fifteen minutes and could not find anything. We decided to start walking home and got back on the path again, we were nearly out of the woods when I turned around and saw behind us, the man with the walking stick watching us leave.

We mentioned it to some friends who live close to the woods and they had seen the man also around Midnight but they saw at one point he was lying down. They thought someone had attacked him but when they ran over to help, nothing was there. When they looked around they couldn't see him anywhere!

THE HOODED FIGURE

Whilst living in the Student Halls in Hull's Old Town, East Yorkshire from September 1998 to June 1999, something bizarre happened to my fellow students and myself.

It all started in my bedroom, when my bed sheet was being pulled from me in the early hours of the morning. I would try to pull the sheet back up to my neck but whatever was pulling was strong. Having gone back to sleep and then going to college in the morning, I had forgotten about the experience.

Nothing happened for a couple of weeks whilst I was sleeping, until I started getting pinned down in bed, totally paralysed. This happened throughout the academic year at random nights. When it happened for the fifth time, I was really angry and I decided to have a look at who or what was doing this to me.

From being paralysed it took so much effort to move my head from facing the wall to four inches to the right facing the ceiling. I could move my eyes; I looked to the right and I saw a roughly seven feet tall, pitch black hooded figure that resembled a monk looking down at me.

The weird thing was that I was frightened but not bothered at the same time, which resulted in me going back to sleep again.

After this experience I started thinking, "is it just me having this?" From asking various friends living in the same building, I soon discovered that about five others had the same experience.

One of my friends dreamt that this black hooded figure was attacking him with a knife and slashing his hands. He woke up crying. My other friend had seen it next to him, like I did, being pinned down in bed. Another person experienced something getting into bed with him whilst he was paralysed and described 'a sharp long nail' doing slow circular movements on his buttock. I had something tickling my ribs whilst being in paralysis, and then it stopped when I broke out of it.

A year later a TV programme was broadcast about our building's grounds and remains of a monastery from the 1100's being discovered – something we didn't know before our experiences.

THE FARNWORTH GHOST BRIDE

This is about a sighting my sister had nearly forty years ago. At the bottom of Cemetery Rd, Farnworth near Bolton there was a strip of land we used to call 'the vat waste'. After crossing this land, you came to the canal near a place called the Stopes, my sister and a group of about seven friends (around seventeen or eighteen years old at the time) kept horses on the farm at the back of the canal.

After returning the horses to the field they sat beside of the canal before commencing on the long walk back into Farnworth. Just chatting amongst one another, they all heard footsteps clattering down the hill from the Stopes.

They all turned to see who it was, and a woman in a wedding dress came running past them and flung herself into the canal! They were horrified and a little in shock I would imagine, but they all ran to the canal to save her. As soon as they saw her, she seemed to jump out of the canal and started running towards Prestolee Road. My sister and her friends were in absolute shock, they checked the side of the canal where the bride jumped out but there was not one drop of water – a big surprise considering she was wearing a wedding dress.

It scared the dickens out of the lot of them I think they made Farnworth in record time that day.

I moved to Canada over thirty years ago and I have yet to find anyone else who has witnessed the bride. It is strange how something like this stays clear in your mind after such a long time ago.

SOUTHEND HAUNTED HOTEL

MJ Wayland writes: Mark B. contacted me about his experiences on Southend sea front from over twenty years ago, "I was playing a game of tag in a burnt out hotel on Southend sea front, (we had a den and all that boy nonsense) and on the top floor was what was once the ballroom, (I think) but the floor had all been burnt away.

I was up there and the only way you could across the room was to carefully step from joist to joist and below was a three story fall into the basement full of rubbish. I was looking out of the window watching my mates running about chasing each other, when I felt someone tap me quite hard on the shoulder and I heard a mans voice say, " its burning".

I turned around and there was no one there. I left in a hurry."

This story was one of many published in a popular online magazine and soon after I was contacted by Harry who had a similar experience in the same hotel.

"Having read Mark's letter regarding his experience at the burnt out Southend seafront hotel, I felt I had to write to you with an experience I had many years ago. It was on the 7th of March 1973 (I know it's sad, but I've kept a diary since 1968!) my girlfriend and I went to Southend for the day. Being only 19 at the time, we thought it adventurous to book into a hotel for the night! Unfortunately the hotel we picked was a bleak looking place called 'Boston Hall Hotel' situated on the sea front, Leigh on Sea end. We spent the evening at the amusements, bought some chips and a can of cola (I know how to treat a girl) and made our way back to the hotel. I specifically remember drinking the rest of my cola in our room and placing it carefully in the metal bin. Anyway, we both fell asleep and about 2:00am we both woke up at the same time feeling quite scared.

The room felt very cold, possibly the time of the year, but we could hear old spinet type music faintly playing seemingly from inside our room. A few moments later, we heard what seemed to be footsteps walking around by the walls of the room. While trying to convince myself and my girlfriend that there must be a rational explanation, we heard a deafening sound of metal to metal. It sounded like someone had thrown my cola can into the bin. This was real and definitely in our room. We put on the lights, got dressed and made our way out of there. On the way out I looked in the bin and the can was still where I had placed it earlier.

About twelve years ago I took my wife to Southend and thought I would show her the "haunted hotel", but when we walked up to it there were

boards all around it and only the frontage seemed to be standing. I
believe this could be the same place Mark had experience only a few
years before. Finally, I thought I would take a souvenir photo of what
was left of the hotel. I took the photo and dropped the camera spilling
the film all over the floor - spooky or not?"

FIRTH PARK SCHOOL GHOST

As a child growing up in Firth Park I was always aware of local ghost stories. One of the most haunted places in Firth Park was Firth Park School situated on Barnsley Road. It was a tall Victorian building built in a blackish stone, and was originally a country home, part of the Brushes Estate.

One night in the late 1970's while walking back from Boys Brigade, we decided to walk past Firth Park School to look for ghosts, we had heard about a phantom teacher who could be seen walking around the classrooms at night. We stood at the school's large iron gates eating our vinegar-moistened chips peering through the school fence for a glimpse of the demon teacher. After what seemed an eternity and anyway we had finished our chips, we started to walk home. One of my friends first heard a screeching coming from the school and told us to shut up to hear it. The noise became louder and we realised the sound was a war siren; even though it seemed distant it was definitely coming from the school. We ran back to the gates of the school and began to look for the ghost again and we saw in the school's central turret about fifty feet high, a silhouette of someone walking around it. We knew that the turret had been blocked off years ago because it was in a dangerous state - the figure had to be a ghost! My friends and I, still with the siren ringing out ran quickly back to our homes as fast as our feet could carry us!

I told my parents about what happened, which they treated with the usual scepticism. The next day when I arrived home, I found our next-door neighbour chatting with my Mother. Mr Hudson, who had lived all his life just one hundred yards from the school confirmed that during World War II the turret was used as look out tower to spot German bombers and fires in Sheffield and furthermore he was sat on his back door step the previous night and had heard the siren too.

THE SHADOW MEN

MJ Wayland writes: Around the millennium I investigated a series of sightings around the country of "shadow men" - ghostly figures with no discernable features.

Steve's sighting was one of many at that time.

"I live in Devon and around October 2001 I was out driving, being only twenty at the time I enjoyed driving around with my friends at night.

We drove into a car park where we go regularly as it is right next to a beach and it is quite long and dark. As I drove towards the end, me and my friend noticed a black flash zoom across the front of a fence at the end of the car park. It sent a shiver down me as I saw it, and my friend and me simultaneously shouted, "Did you see that?" The car's head lamps helped to show the object in the light - it was very black and moved very fast. I drove over to where it was but we did not see anything else, we just thought it might have been a bat or something like that, or a fox creating a large shadow in the light of the head lamps.

A few weeks later I found myself driving into the same car park with a different friend. Again it was dark and empty so I drove right to the end of the car park and stopped. I really needed to go to the toilet, so I walked over a bank about ten metres from the car. My friend waited in the car alone, and when I got back he said, "Umm I've just been watching a black human-shaped object moving slowly over the other side of the car park". I thought he was joking but he wasn't. I told him about my sighting and it sounded very similar.

I don't know what it is and I have been there lots of times but I have only seen the black thing once. Maybe I will see it again one day - I shall keep watching."

A week later I received another witness experience of a "shadow man".

John wrote to me, "I saw something just like Steve's experience in my backyard once. It was a few years ago, I was about twelve years old. I was taking out the trash to my backyard. There is a light on each corner of my house, one was in front of me (but not really pointing at me) and the other was behind me. I was walking toward the big trashcan (where the trash went) when I saw it.

It was just a solid black being, about an average adult male height, maybe a little shorter. I could not tell if it was actually a male or not, because you couldn't really see any depth to it because it was solid black. The light partially shone on to it but it just seemed to absorb the light. I stopped as soon as I saw it, but it continued walking from my left to my right. There was a chain-link fence behind the big trash can, and I could see the "shadow man" was on my side of it, walking beside it. I don't remember it's exact movements, but I think it looked in my direction for a second (kind of reminds me of that bigfoot film), and then turned slightly away from me. This is when I really knew that it wasn't a shadow because it walked straight through the fence and into the dark. I am not sure our two experiences are connected, seeing how I live in South - Eastern USA."

THE CRASH WATCHER

MJ Wayland writes: this experience was sent to me after the "Shadow man" article was published. The story sounds fantastic, and scary however I did not receive further communications from the witness, so I have my doubts how true it is. As a ghost story, it's enjoyable and scary at the same time.

"My story begins in the autumn of 1984. I was six years old and I only just remember the chain of events, my elder brother remembers this part much better than myself.

My father had picked us up from school and we were driving towards a town called Whitham, in Essex. He needed to get some cash so he could take us swimming. He pulled the car over round the corner from the bank and left us while he went inside. About ten seconds after he left, a man opened the passenger door and got in. My brother and I sat silent and scared, he was wearing some kind of black wrap around his head and just sat there looking straight ahead faintly mumbling something.

Suddenly there was a loud crash and I looked past the man out of the front windscreen and saw that two cars had collided at the junction ahead. At this point the man opened the car door and got out, I was crying and did not see what happened to him and my brother was trying to comfort me. My father doubted our story.

In May 2001 my father phoned me. He said he had been crossing the road in a town called Colchester. As he reached the other side of the road he noticed a badly parked car, as he walked past the side of it along the pavement to his amazement he recognised the black wrapped figure sitting in the passenger seat. It was the one we had described all those years ago - he said he just froze. He was jolted out of this by a loud banging noise, and looked across the junction to see a three-car pile up taking place. When he looked back to the car the door was open but the figure had gone, and sitting in the back was a crying five-year-old boy.

Two weeks later, at the start of June, my brother was driving through Gloucester. He stopped at a red light and saw the figure sitting in a parked car about ten yards away. Fearing the worst, when the lights went green he put on his emergency indicators and did not move. Three cars from behind passed him, honking their horns and the fourth went straight into the back of him.

I think I have witnessed him on about five occasions, but I can't be certain. I also think I have seen him in the background of TV news reports. He's about six foot tall and the black wrap around his head covers his eyes and all. He wears a black tunic which joins the head wrap and there is something under his tunic on his back, almost like he's got a pair of folded wings underneath, yet somehow he blends in, it's almost like you don't want to notice him."

THE GHOST OF GIBBET LANE

Whittington Common, Stourbridge is the area where the ghost of William Howe is believed to haunt, he was hanged on a gibbet in a near-by wood for the murder of a local farmer.

As for the ghost experience, myself and two friends used to go on long walks during the summer months, just to get away from town. We all knew the legend of the "gibbet wood" ghost, so one evening we decided to walk to Kinver, taking a short cut on Gibbet Lane from the Stourbridge side. The lane is nothing more than a badly pot-holed unsurfaced road, running through the middle of the woods about a mile and a half in length.

It was getting fairly dark and this is not a place frequented by people at night generally! At about 9.45pm, about half way through the woods, the three of us stopped in our tracks overcome with an overwhelming sense of dread, anger and being watched from all around. Prior to this we were happily talking and even forgot about the haunting. We looked at each other in the fading light and somehow we knew we could all feel this horrible sensation without saying it!

Eventually I said, "Ok lets just keep going, it is getting dark, we'll just get out the other side and walk home along the main road." We emerged from the woods and continued the last few hundred yards to the end of the lane where it meets the main road to Kidderminster.

We stopped for a rest for a few minutes where we reflected on what happened. We just couldn't explain the feeling we had or why we stopped in our tracks at the same time.

My friend said, "It is going to take ages to get home if we walk the main roads, lets just turn round and go back. There is nothing there it was just a coincidence that we all stopped."

We all agreed and by this time it was dark, I was quite shaken inside but didn't want to tell my two friends, as they seemed to have shrugged it off. We set off back towards the wood and I began to feel more at ease and "young lads" conversation made me forget what happened before.

It was a clear night and there was just enough moonlight to see ahead of us without falling down a pothole! We reached a point where the lane inclines and bares round to the left slightly, as we walked round this point, we instinctively went very quiet and our walking pace slowed right down

I whispered, "There is someone walking towards us, can you see?"

My friend said, "its just the branches moving or your eyes playing tricks.

I realised that my friend was wrong and shouted, "no, that is definitely someone walking towards us!"

We all stopped and looked ahead of the moonlit path and could see someone coming towards us at a very fast pace.

At that moment everything around us seemed to go into a weird silence, we stood frozen watching the figure of a man about six feet tall and about a hundred yards ahead of us. We could see that he was wearing headwear, something like a tricorn and had a long cloak or jacket.

The same feeling we had before was upon us and this time we all agreed this wasn't some trick of the dark, there was no doubt a tall man approaching us.

All this happened within the space of ten to twenty seconds although it seemed like time had stopped. At this point we turned back and ran from the woods back to the main road home.
I do not know whether we experienced a "real person" walking through the woods, a trick of the imagination based on what we knew of the area or that it was a genuine apparition, I really can't say for sure. One thing is certain, that my friends and I have never ventured on to the path since.

WHITTINGTON COMMON GHOST

MJ Wayland writes, I wouldn't usually do this, but I thought I would include a ghost experience from 1872. It provides a great comparison of what was experienced at Gibbet Lane one hundred thirty years ago, compared to what you have just read in "The Ghost of Gibbet Lane". The witnesses to the previous story only knew about the alleged ghost of a "hanged man" and did not know the details of this earlier sighting.

"Perhaps you will afford me space to give a short narrative of an adventure which occurred while crossing Whittington Common, which people who are acquainted with the locality know is lonely place at night. I had been to Kinver and remained rather longer that I intended, and about half past eleven passed the Whittington Inn. In two minutes or so I was in the solitude of the Common. With the silence around me I was on guard in case I should be surprised or set upon by some desparate character, but let no one suppose I was oppressed by the silence or solitariness. No such thing, I was enjoying the solitariness and drinking delight from the wonderous beauty and calmness of the scene and jogging along at something like three miles an hour. From the time of leaving Kinver I had not met a single soul, but at this moment just as I was about to ascend a hill - I observed a figure approaching.

Its manner of approach struck me as strange, it appeared rather to glide than walk, but I accounted for this by the softness of the ground which prevented me hearing the footfalls. At this moment the moon was overshadowed and a comparative darkness fell upon the scene. There however, the figure still stood, and I could see it plainly although the moon was obscured. I demanded why I was thus stopped, but there was no answer and I made an attempt to pass on one side. I was far from feeling assured that I could force a passage and raising my stick with all my force aimed a blow at the unwelcome visitor. My blow was well aimed but my stick passed straight through what ought to have been a head. The swing made me stumble and I heard a low chuckling laugh. The figure extended a long arm and I was pressed gently and irresistibly down until I was laid upon my back on the wayside. A cold sweat broke out and the phantom continued to stand a yard away. I could see it with perfect distinction as the cloud had passed from the moon and she was again pouring a silver stream over everything around.

At last day began to break, and as the first ray gilded the clouds on the eastern horizon the phantom lifted up both its arms over its shadowy head, uttered once again its mocking chuckle, and disappeared.

I felt immediate deliverance and reached home in a complete state of exhaustion, mental and physical. I can only say that I never get drunk and was perfectly sober. Moreover, no dreams visit the bestial sleep of the drunkard. Others will say that I must be a timid man and that my imagination played me a trick. To this I would say that I am not of timorous nature and my health was never better at the time. How to account for the adventure I cannot tell, but I shall not forget the experience of that horrible night."

Ref: 14th December 1872 - Brierley Hill and Stourbridge Advertiser

MIDLAND HOTEL, MORECAMBE

The Midland Hotel, Morecambe has recently been restored to its original 1920's Art Deco glamour. In 1987 I used to work at the hotel as a security night watchman. Once while on duty I was sat in the lounge reading a newspaper, suddenly I was disturbed by the sound of footsteps on a tiled surface when no one was supposed to be on the ground floor. My attention was immediate, the footsteps then changed from tile to carpet, but as I was sat in the lounge the footsteps then began to pass from left to right with no one in sight.

Later that week I was playing on a video game machine in that same corridor the footsteps were heard, now bear in mind that I had been playing this to pass the time.

I had played on the arcade machine all week, trying to beat my score every time I played. I had reached the difficult levels and a new high score when I felt the temperature drop, and I felt as if someone was looking over my shoulder.

I quickly looked over my shoulder but there was no one there so I just ran away leaving the machine to it's own devices.

Another strange occurrence happened that week while I was in the elevator.

From the third floor, instead of taking me to the ground floor it took me to the darkened basement, which scared me a lot. I pressed the button to the upper floors. I stood staring into the basement's darkness half expecting something to jump out at me, luckily for me nothing did. I later found out that the basement was used as a morgue during World War II.

THE RIVOCK EDGE GHOST

David Key, a council countryside worker based in Riddlesden, Lancashire saw an apparition in March 1998.

Working as a part of the drainage and resurfacing team at the plantation in Rivock Edge, he saw a figure float just a hundred yards in front of him. When we interviewed him he said, "it was grey and hooded, I went over to the point where it had been but there was no sign of anything. Whatever I saw floated, no human could have done that. It was frightening."

After his experience, other workers on the project admitted they had also experienced the same phenomenon just months earlier. Malcolm Leyland told us about when he had seen a ghostly figure in the plantation about seven months later. He was walking through the site when he saw what appeared to be the spectre of a man drifting across the path.

Malcolm told us, "I never mentioned it to anybody because I didn't want to appear an idiot. I am very sceptical about ghosts but I saw something that day."

At the time the countryside service was resurfacing ancient bridleways in the area, the path that runs through Rivock Edge was an ancient packhorse route nearly seven hundred years old.

Did David and Malcolm witness the ghost of an ancient traveller?

THE OLD BARN GHOST

In the town which I live in Worcestershire, there is an old barn conversion owned by the town council. It is hired out solely for functions but has also had a playgroup there for years.

Anyway at the back of the building is a small room which has been converted to a kitchen. I always remember that the room was always freezing cold, even if the heating and all the cooking points were on full blast.

One day my mother was working at the playgroup and had to go up a flight of stairs to a cupboard above said room. After getting what she needed she closed the cupboard door and turning round jumped with shock on finding an oddly dressed figure stood on the stairs.

Apologising she asked the man what he was doing and looked him up and down, all the while a niggling odd feeling at the back of her mind. It was only after looking him up and down again she realised what was bothering her. The man's lower legs were missing almost as if he was standing on a different level. She screamed, he vanished, she screamed again and ran out of the building.

When my mother returned to the building she told her fellow workers about her experience. A few moments later the owner of the farmhouse behind the hall entered the building to see what had happened.

The farmer's wife told them about something much more ghostly that had happened to her. Because of the mud she often wore large heavy-duty boots when outside and when she came in she left them on newspaper. One day she was in the kitchen when she heard heavy footfalls coming down the corridor. She ignored them but on leaving the room she found muddy footprints and the boots next to the kitchen doorway. Annoyed she put them back, on the belief that it was her children messing around, and continued what she was doing in the kitchen. Needless to say the same thing happened again, so putting them back, she decided to catch the culprit in the act.

So when she heard the footfalls she stepped out only to find the boots walking down the corridor on their own accord which stopped dead in front of the wall.

Obviously frightened it led her to investigate what could possibly be the cause of the ghostly goings on. She discovered that during the Civil War, King Charles had hidden in the barn but had been discovered.

Though he escaped all of his loyal supporters there were massacred in cold blood by a roundhead regiment.

THE BREWERY HAUNTING

For many years during the 1970s and 1980s I was PR manager at Manns and Norwich Brewery in Northampton. Over the years I came to know The Daventry Express photographer Pete Spencer well. One day he called me about a pub at Braunston called the Admiral Nelson.

At that time, the brewery had just started an extensive refurbishment programme, which involved some structural changes inside the bar. Pete had heard on the grapevine that several customers had reported seeing a ghostly presence during the time the building work was being done.

I spoke to the landlord who confirmed what Pete had heard and said there had been a number of sightings. Several were from people who had never been in the pub before – but all described a man in period costume with a blackened face a bit like a chimney sweep, with dirty clothes and a sooty appearance.

The landlord showed us where the sightings had occurred and Pete took some pictures. We had a drink together, Pete and I had a laugh in the car park about ghosts, and we set off back to our respective offices.

Later that day Pete called me. He said he had just developed the pictures, and all had a large black smudge. A smudge he couldn't account for and was in exactly the same spot where the black-faced man had been seen. All this happened so long ago I'm afraid I can't remember the year, or the licensee's name. But I wonder if Pete remembers the day he took those photos?

ENCOUNTERS WITH GHOSTS

Laura has had several extraordinary encounters in the United Kingdom, sometimes with other witnesses, and others by herself. She contacted me to tell me about some of her strange experiences at a few well known haunted locations.

December 17, 1997
I once had an experience in Borley Church, opposite the site of Borley Rectory, once known as the most haunted house in England. My friend and I drove from her home in Newmarket to Borley, it was mid-afternoon on a very clear, bright and cold December day. Since there was nothing to see of the rectory, we decided to walk around the church.
Unfortunately, when we tried to go inside, the front door was padlocked. My friend was not feeling well and it was very cold, so she returned to sit in the car while I spent a little time looking at the graves and walking around the exterior of the church. I noticed nothing unusual and at the point, I didn't know very much about phenomena occurring at the church and photographs I took and later developed showed nothing out of the ordinary.

However, while I was walking around the outside of the church, near the wall, I heard voices singing from inside - like a choir practicing. In fact, that's what I thought, "Oh, the choir must be practicing." It took me a moment to remember that the church was padlocked - from the outside. There was no one in the church at the time I heard the singing. I've since read that other visitors to the church have heard the sounds of singing.

September 8, 1995
Middleham Castle, Yorkshire: While on holiday with a friend from Cumbria, I visited the castle when it first opened in the morning, and walked about filming the interior walls and buildings, most of which are in ruins. While I was in the round tower, known as the Prince's Tower - the site of the medieval nursery, I heard a newborn baby wailing. The sound was caught on tape. The crying seemed to come from somewhere other than the Prince's Tower, so I hurried out and went to see if there was an actual child crying. The only other visitors that morning besides my friend and myself were a young couple with two children - one of which was about five and the other about three. They were nowhere near the tower when I heard the child's cry. Also, it was very definitely a newborn baby's cry, not a young child. I have not read of any instances of ghostly phenomena at Middleham Castle, despite its great age and associations with Richard III among others.

Spring, 1994

Tewkesbury was the site of a very bloody fight between the Yorkists and the Lancastrians in the mid fifteenth century. The historical records say that several Lancastrians fled to sanctuary in the church and were murdered there by Yorkist soldiers. The church was not technically a cathedral but an abbey, the Yorkists considered the right of sanctuary not to apply. One of the interior doors is 'veneered' with pieces of metal said to be armour and have been recovered by monks from the Abbey from the battlefield.

There is a small room or chapel at the end of the nave and in the corner, that feels very, very bad. I don't know how else to describe it. I sat alone in this room for quite a while - a very oppressive atmosphere and I had the sense of someone hiding in this room and fearing for their lives.

The church was re-consecrated in the fifteenth century after the battle, but I think some of the spirits of the men who were killed there are still there. In fact, George of Clarence - brother of Richard III and Edward IV, who was famously murdered for political treason by being drowned in a butt of Malmsey wine, is buried in a crypt below the floor.

HAUNTED HOUSE IN NEWFOUNDLAND

I should like to share with you some experiences of my husband and myself that fall into the realm of the paranormal. I should explain that we live in Newfoundland, where talk of "The Good People" and ghosts and such are the usual thing at parties and whatnot.

About ten years ago, my husband and I inherited a Victorian house (built 1893) from my husband's uncle, who had just passed on. We had cared for him whilst he was ill, and, although he had been something of a recluse for most of his life, he became rather close to me during his final days.

Some other family members were in dispute about whether my husband and I ought to inherit Uncle Mike's house, and for a time it looked as though we would have to remain in our very small apartment. Always an optimistic person, I began moving some of our belongings into "Mike's House" in hopes that things would turn out for the best.

Well, one sunny afternoon, not long after Uncle Mike had passed on, I unlocked the front door of the house and Mike was sitting on the chesterfield! I had always been able to 'see" ghosts and spirits, since I was a small child, and I wasn't frightened. He told me that he would remain in the house until he was certain it had passed into our hands, and that he wanted us to love it as much as he had. True to his word, he stayed in the house for three weeks exactly, until we had the papers drawn up by a solicitor, and the house passed into our hands. On the day we moved in officially, Uncle Mike was gone. It was as if he had been looking out for us.

Another interesting thing occurred in this house one cold January evening. My husband had been watching the television in our bedroom whilst I attended an evening class, just up the street. I wear glasses, and as I came in from the cold, I had to remove them. As I walked up the stairs, I glanced up into the other room, which is my study, and saw what I thought was my husband in his pyjamas. I couldn't figure out why on earth he would be in the darkened room at this hour of the night - it was close to eleven! As I got closer, I saw that it was the figure of a woman, in Victorian dress, holding a lamp. I opened my mouth to say something to her, and her form grew thin and vanished. It's interesting to note that other visitors to my house have seen the figure of a woman in white going up the stairs, and our dog has often sat staring and growling at the staircase, when there isn't anything there.

We have other ghosts here in this house: a pair of children, a boy and girl, who appear in Victorian clothing, holding hands. They most commonly appear at the side of our bed, and aren't in any way threatening, but merely curious, or so it seems. My husband awoke one night to see the children standing by the side of the bed, gazing at him.

JoAnne Soper-Cook
St. John's, Newfoundland

OXFORD STREET GHOST

About three or four years ago, during a nice bright summer, I was doing some research at Oriel College. Around lunchtime I was hungry so left the building to get some food.

After eating, as it was a nice day I decided to take a walk around. I believe the location I ended up was Holywell Street, or that area. It was a long wide straight street that appeared to be closed off by some white fencing across the road to prevent traffic access onto what appeared to be water meadows. I was aware the main part of the city was to my right (to the south). There was a high wall along the street on that side. I had walked to the end and turned and was on my back, the wall now to my left.

I came to a part where there was an alleyway to my left which had a pub or restaurant along it. At this point, I became aware of a man walking towards me, who was certainly very noticeable and out of place by his appearance. He was about forty feet or so from me and I would describe him as a large man, about six feet five inches, broad shouldered, narrow waisted and very tanned. He had shoulder length black hair, pageboy style and a short tidy beard, goatee style.

His clothing is what made him look odd. He had on his head an alpine hat made of felt or suede with possibly a peacock feather sticking out of it. A very voluminous shirt with long sleeves which looked as if it was made of a cream coloured silk, open at the neck to halfway down his chest, no fastenings were seen so presume the shirt was put on over the head. He had on a sleeveless jacket or jerkin that looked as if it was made of brown suede. Trousers were tight like leggings coloured a dark browny grey, and seemed to be made of thick wool. His shoes were made of suede leather, no soles or heels but seemingly wrapped around the feet and tied with narrow strips of leather for laces, the shoes were pointed at the toes. He had on a brown leather belt with a large buckle. Tied to the front on the man's right side, was a leather purse/pouch. The man looked completely real and solid. I took him to possibly be an actor from a theatre who was taking a break, though it would have taken a lot of courage for him to walk around Oxford city like that at about 1:30pm on a weekday.

As the man walked past me, from the back, he had a knife/dagger tucked into his belt on the right side of his hip/backside, aged about the mid-thirties. Up to this point, nothing caused me to consider I was watching something that may have not existed. It all looked so real, but then I looked at the other people on the street and there was quite a few, I realised that no one else appeared to have noticed him. I looked back down the street towards the white fencing and he had disappeared.

Having only just walked along from there I knew there was nowhere he could have gone to, he had simply vanished.

I still think long and hard about this experience. I believe I saw the ghost of what can only be described as a fourteenth century well-to-do male who walked out of his time into mine and then walked back out of it.

WESTBOURNE HOUSE HOTEL

Having read your book I wanted to tell you about my experiences that I felt when my girlfriend (at the time) and I stayed at a Hotel in the Broomhill area of Sheffield. We were both students in the city and as a treat after our exams we decided to have a meal in a restaurant and stay in a hotel. I found a hotel in the 'Yellow Page's called Westbourne House Hotel, on Westbourne Road and rang to book a room. When the day arrived we were both in high spirits (finishing our exams) and booked into the hotel and were led downstairs to our room. As the hotel (like most places in Sheffield) was situated on a hill the main entrance to the building was on the second level of the five on Westbourne Road. Our room was on the ground floor (one below main reception floor) opening out to the garden at the back of the property. The room was great, we quickly changed and went out for our meal.

On returning to the hotel (still in very high spirits) we made our way down the stairs from the main reception to our room. As soon as we got into the room our moods changed to a sombre/depressed state. After a few exchanges we decided to call it a night and go to bed - I remember being very tired and falling to sleep straight away, only to be awaken by my girlfriend sat-up in bed crying. Asking her what was a matter she firstly gave me a strange look then went on to explain that I had been talking and swearing at her in my sleep in a very low, rough voice.

On hearing this I was very confused, scared and shocked - I just didn't understand what I'd done or said? She was confused because I just couldn't remember saying anything. The really worrying part about it is I had my eyes open at the time. We discussed the incident the next day and her explanation of my voice and my eyes being open at the time was weird. I felt very disappointed that I had ruined the night but just couldn't remember saying or doing anything. OK - I'll admit we had alcohol that night, a bottle of wine with a our meal, (that's all we could afford) but I'm convinced something weird happened in the room. The mood change, feeling sleepy then waking up to my girlfriend crying explaining that I'd been swearing at her in a low voice with my eyes open.

After graduating and working around the South East for the past five years, I now live and work in Sheffield and sometimes drive past Westbourne House Hotel. I still feel something weird about the place. I have never had anything like that happen to me before or since.

HORROR AT HUNDRED HOUSE HOTEL

I was staying on my own in the Hundred House Hotel in Telford, Shropshire whilst away on business, the room I was in was quite comfortably appointed.

I felt a little uneasy, there was some atmosphere about the room and when the lights went out to get to sleep, more so. I was there for three or four nights and don't think I went fully to sleep the whole time.

It was second or third night I cannot quite recall now, that the most disturbing things occurred. I was woken from my fitful sleep by a distinct slap on my buttock. Naturally this woke me up sharply. I put on the lights rapidly but there was no one else in the room. Disturbingly what caught my eye was the "love seat" or swing suspended by two chains from the ceiling in my room was gently swinging back and forth probably about four inches.

I'm not sure why I didn't leave the room, but I didn't.

Perhaps my mind just didn't want to believe what was happening. Sitting upright in the bed still, I could hear faint sound of a bell intermittently. Was it the nearby church I wondered - unlikely at approx 3:00am in the morning. I later recalled the large brass bell, like a ships bell, in the reception area, used to announce your arrival at check in and last orders.

It was like the bell was being blown gently back and forth rather than someone deliberately ringing it. This went on intermittently. The next disturbing occurrence was the dressing table at the right hand side of my bed started to vibrate the objects resting on its surface.

With that I put on every light I could find and the TV on wishing for morning to arrive ASAP. I slept with all the lights on for my remaining nights there. I do not know if the area is renowned for seismic activity which could explain some of the phenomena. I felt a bit embarrassed about broaching the matter with the owner. I didn't think he would appreciate the possibility of scaring away trade.

However I did risk the ridicule of my work colleagues I was on training with by mentioning my experiences of the night. I tried to pre-empt ridicule by making light of it myself by dubbing it the phantom arse-slapper room. On my last night or penultimate (cannot recall which) stay, as I was dosing off, it happened again! I felt a slap or contact on my leg or buttock (cannot recall exactly where) which again awoke me. I don't recall any other of the aforementioned phenomena occurring that time.

PELSALL ROAD GHOST

It was broad daylight as I was travelling alone on the Wolverhampton Road in Pelsall, Walsall. I was travelling towards Pelsall from Brownhills and had gone over the last canal bridge.

As I was approaching a bend in the road I saw a woman standing very close to the edge of the curb. I remember distinctly thinking to myself, "she should get back its dangerous standing there".

I was following an articulated lorry at the time and as the lorry went around the bend in the road it obscured my line of vision with this woman. As the lorry drove past this point the woman had gone. I checked through both windows and could see no sign of her. It concerned me that much that I slowed down to turn round to check through the back window and could not see her.

At the point where she was crossing there was nothing but bushes and a fence for her to cross to, there was no path and she did not have time to run back from the road to hide! She was of average height and very slim build. She was dressed in clothes from the 1960's and a pale Mac that was tied tightly at the waist and brown shoes. She had red hair that was loosely permed and very full. I did not see her face as she was looking directly ahead all the time.

MJ Wayland writes, the area around Pelsall is particularly haunted with many sightings through the years of strange shadowy figures. The Pelsall Road is noted as one of the oldest roads in the county and has been in use for over five hundred years.

HILLBANK HOTEL AND ARROWE PARK HAUNTINGS

I have had a couple of experiences that have left me shaken up and convinced that ghosts are a part of a science we do not yet understand. I had a terribly frightening experience at a place called Hillbark Hotel, Royden Park. The house was built originally in 1891 and had been moved from it's original site and rebuilt brick by brick approximately seven miles away on the site of an old tithe barn.

It has a rather imposing mock Tudor edifice, but not what you would imagine as spooky in any way. Following the death of it's owner in 1961, the house became a mental health facility for older people who had developed senile dementia. My office was a lovely sunny room, located through an oak panelled hidden doorway.

I had the residents participate in occupational therapy, and while I was in a room waiting for the staff to bring someone in, I had a feeling that there was somebody in the room with me. I couldn't see anything, but I knew I wasn't alone. I turned away from the room and looked through the window out over the gardens. It was a bright day and yet I was cold to the bone.

The staff were very busy that day and it took over an hour for one of the nurses to bring someone into me. In all that time I stayed frozen, looking out at the gardens. I couldn't turn around. When I questioned the other staff, I found out that I was not alone in experiencing this. As my job at the time allowed me to move from facility to facility, I chose not to return to Hillbark. It is now a conference centre and hotel.

However, my next job was in a home for the physically disabled and was in an old house in Arrowe Park, Upton. This home had once allegedly belonged to a member of the Hellfire club and the house's huge furnishings are now kept in the Birkenhead museum. The carved wood fireplaces and various pieces are covered with imps, demons and fairy folk.

When the house was being refurbished, the builders found a pentagram on the floor of the hallway. It measured about twenty feet in diameter. Anyway, there is a spiral staircase that the care assistants used to leave their belongings and no one would change there alone as it was rumoured that there was a ghost there. I never felt anything untoward there, but in another part of the building I did see a little girl pass by the doorway of one of the rooms. When I poked my head out through the

door there was nobody there. It was a long empty corridor. All the
rooms off it had to be unlocked with keys and used only for storage.

GHOSTS OF HANGMAN'S HILL, EPPING FOREST

I have spent my teenage years in the surrounding areas of the well-known Epping Forest in Essex. My mates and me have often ventured out into the forest at day and night and I have always felt safe there. There is an area of the forest called High Beech and in the forest is a place unofficially named Hangman's Hill. Legend has it that if you park on the hill the car will roll up it instead of down and as you reach the top, look straight ahead you will see a bare field with just a tree in it – this is apparently where a man was hung, supposedly you are being pulled up the hill by the hangman.

Many of my friends say it is an optical illusion but have always been so scared by the experience they have never got out of the car to see if they are actually on a hill.

Last weekend we decided to look for Hangman's Hill as no one can remember it's exact location and probably didn't want to. We must have been driving through the forest for hours, but could not find the tiny slip road. I turned into one of the bigger roads which I know quite well. As I was driving down it I saw something standing in the middle of the road, it looked like a man flagging us down for help. We did not want to stop for him so carried on driving, we got closer and closer and he wouldn't move out of the way. I stopped right in front of him thinking he must really be in trouble but couldn't see him properly so I switched my lights to full beam.

The man just turned and ran away. We presumed it was a joke and drove out of the forest.

I persuaded my boyfriend to take me down there the next night to look for the Hangman's Hill as his navigation talents are better than mine, we couldn't find it, so my boyfriend parked outside a pub and went in to ask for directions.

Whilst I waited in a car I noticed a man running towards the car from down the road, it was the same man I had seen the night before! My boyfriend got back into the car and I turned to him to point out the man and on turning back the man once again disappeared.

Another Hangman's Hill Experience

Just thought I'd share my experiences with you.

"Since I was about twelve years old I've heard stories about a place in High Beech, Epping Forest called "Hangman's Hill" so one night me and my friend got in his car and decided to take a drive up there.

We asked a local about the legend and he told us about what had happened up Hangman's Hill. We went to the hill and my friend stopped his car. After a few seconds the car started to roll, I thought it was my friend joking about until I realised his car was off. I decided to get out to see what happened, when I did, I felt very cold being it was one of the hottest summers we've had I found this very odd.

After a few seconds I saw what seemed to be a shadow of a man standing in the woods and he was staring right at my friend's car then looked directly at me and smiled.

As I watched him I realised he seemed to be making a pulling motion. I asked my friend if he could see him but he couldn't. When I went to get back into his car I heard a laugh which seemed to echo throughout the woods. Me and my friend drove off after that, I looked back and could still see the man standing there, possibly waiting for the next car or person to go to Hangman's Hill.

The one thing that I've always wondered about that night is what would have happened had I not gotten back in the car?"

GHOST OF THE CHAPEL

When I was first married (twenty four years ago) I lived in a small council flat near to an old chapel called Zoar Chapel dated around 1830. My husband, who was a big formidable man, used to laugh at ghost stories. Until, that is one snowy wintry morning he saw one himself! It was around 5:00am, he awoke to get ready to go to work and peered over to our baby son's cot. I was still asleep when he gasped for me to get up and put the light on, which I did urgently, thinking there was something wrong.

I looked at him for an explanation, when he asked me if I could "see her" too? I saw no one. It was then he said there was a bride, dressed in an old fashion bridal gown staring at him. By the pallor of his face I knew he wasn't joking. After a few seconds she disappeared leaving him considerably shaken.

Not being native to the village of Pontlottyn, I started to ask neighbours if any other occupants had seen the phantom bride? I was told that in the chapel's early years a bride was stabbed to death on it's steps after her wedding, by a love rival she had jilted. To end, my husband saw her several times but she never ever put in an appearance to myself.

A GHOST ATTACKED MY BROTHER

This experience happened to my brother about a year ago. My brother has quite a small bedroom, and he doesn't like to sleep in there because it gets very hot. He cannot open the windows because they broke a little while ago. Anyway he decided to sleep on the couch downstairs. He doesn't mind doing this, because then this way, he gets to stay up all night watching telly without my Dad knowing.

It was quite late about half ten when he heard noises coming from the kitchen. It sounded like scratching. My brother thought it was one of the cats, so he thought nothing of it but he huddled up anyway. It was a few minutes later when he heard a bang on the arm of the couch where his head was. It made him jump, and he was so terrified he put his head under the covers and decided to stay like it for the rest of the night. He wanted to go upstairs and go into his room, but he was terrified in case he saw something, so he stayed there.

He tried going back to sleep, but he found it hard. He turned over onto his stomach and buried his head under the covers, that's when he felt it. He said it felt like someone was sitting on his legs, and he couldn't move them, they were stuck. He said it was a really heavy weight and it wouldn't budge.

He was so scared he tried calling out, but nothing would come out. He burst out crying. It was then that my mum walked in from a night out with her friends and found my brother crying and shaking. He told her what happened and he said that the weight only lifted when my mum walked into the room.

The next morning when my brother told me I thought he was making it up, because, he is known for not telling the truth but my mum said she knew he wasn't lying this time. When he went up to his bed he couldn't stop crying and was shaking all over. He's never slept downstairs till this day.

BERWICK'S HAUNTED HOUSE

When I was about three years old, my parents moved into a house in Berwick-upon-Tweed. It was a large detached, sandstone building on the outskirts of the town.

My mother was very uncomfortable living in the house and she even told me that she didn't want to buy the house due to her feelings. Often she would feel watched wherever she went in the building, however since we had moved to Berwick to start a new life, and Dad had settled in his new job, she tried to ignore it.

Soon after moving to the house my parents were getting ready to go out to a dinner dance. My mother was sitting at her dressing table, doing her makeup, when she saw in the mirror a figure standing just behind my father. It was of an elderly man, and he seemed to be reading over my father's shoulder, as my father read a book. My mother spun around, shouted, "Arthur!" (my father) but the figure disappeared.

In about the same time period my cousin came to stay for a few days. I am an only child but my parents gave me a bunk bed to sleep in as my cousins came to stay so often.

One night we were lying in bed when the entire bed began to shake. It was as if someone very powerful had a hold of it and was rocking it for all it was worth. Naturally the usual accusations were flung back and forth.

I sat up on the edge of the upper bunk, with all my limbs in sight to him to prove I wasn't doing the shaking. My cousin screamed and ran to my parent's bedroom. With him gone, and the bed still shaking, I quickly followed suit...

Strangely, my parents didn't make much fuss about having two kids join them in bed for the rest of the night. It was about twenty years later that my mother told me that they had both experienced the same bed shaking just a few nights previously.

The strangest thing was to come much later. The room in which I slept when I was a child was next to the guest room. Occasionally I would hear unexplainable sounds coming from it in the dead of night. These would comprise of thumps and bangs, footsteps etc. The first time that I heard these sounds I went next door to investigate but there was no explanation to their cause. From that time on when I heard the noises I'm sorry to admit, I hid under the bed-covers. (Oh come on I was only about ten years old!)

One night my uncle was sleeping in the guest room. He awoke to see the figure of an elderly woman appear out of the fireplace (seemingly) at the foot of the bed. She leaned over him and demanded that he say the Lord's Prayer. My uncle, not religious at the best of times, was absolutely terrified and started praying, at which point the ghost disappeared. The next morning, my uncle told us about his experience, which we all took with a pinch of salt as he has a bit of a reputation as both a prankster and a drinker. It became a bit of a family joke in fact.

About fifteen years later, my uncle and mother were shopping in Berwick when they bumped into the woman who had previously owned the house and her daughter. They all went for coffee, and almost the first thing that the daughter asked was, "have you seen the ghost of the old woman who comes out of the fireplace and demands that you say the lord's prayer?"

It transpires that the house didn't have all that happy a history. A previous owner was the manager of the local slaughter works and killed himself with a humane killer. Sometime in the 1800s the cook in the house had gassed herself in the kitchen.

I don't know if she was the ghost that my uncle saw (it seems unlikely as the ghost was dressed in fashionable Victorian garb) but my mother believes that the house was badly haunted until we moved in. Gradually afterwards, the normalcy and happiness of our family helped to lay the ghosts or at least that is what seemed to happen.

A FRIEND'S HAUNTED HOUSE

I had a paranormal experience in my friend's house of which at the time I didn't know was haunted.

I was still at school at the time and my Dad used to meet me at dinner, this particular day he took me to his friend's house. We had just arrived and I didn't feel right, I had a strange feeling and after a while I went to the toilet.

When I was inside the toilet I could hear someone moving around outside the door and I shouted but no one answered. All of a sudden the door handle went crazy as though someone was desperate to get inside, I shouted again and still no answer. The door handle was still going crazy and then suddenly it stopped. I waited and began to wonder whether I should run downstairs or shout for help. I started shouting. No one came so I plucked up the courage to run downstairs but when I tried the door it was locked! I pulled as hard as I could and the door flew open and I ran down the stairs as quickly as I could, never looking back.

When I got downstairs I was hysterical, I told my Dad and his friend what happened but they just looked at each other. My Dad's friend explained that they didn't want to say anything to me but the house is haunted.

A little while after moving into the house they began to hear a baby crying upstairs only when they reached the top of the staircase it stopped. Often items would go missing from the house and be found the next day in the middle of the garden.

One day when Dad's friend and his brother returned to the house they heard banging and moving around upstairs. They thought it was Sarah, his girlfriend but two minutes later she walked in through the front door, back from work.

Quickly they ran upstairs thinking a burglar was in the house but strangely all the lights were switched on and Sarah's clothes were thrown all about their bedroom. The bath was full of water and the bathroom had items thrown all over the floor. They tidied up the rooms and decided to go out for a pizza switching off all the lights in the house.

When they returned the lights were all back on! After this they asked a priest to bless the house but this did not stop the activity. They moved to another house and have not experienced anything like they have at this haunted house.

REG HAS RETURNED

We first moved into our house in 1990 and from day one, things started to happen. We would return home and the heating would be turned off, the TV and video would be unplugged. On the odd occasion we found the TV switched on in our bedroom when we know for certain that it was off before we went out.

We tried to ignore what was going on at first, we even tried to blame each other for doing the things and forgetting we had done them. This worked for a while until my niece and her boyfriend looked after our house while we were away. My niece on several occasions felt someone touch her on the shoulder and heard the odd muffled bang from upstairs, needless to say they didn't offer to stay again when we were away.

On another occasion we had some friends round for dinner, after eating we all sat chatting in the sitting room when we heard a terrible bang from the kitchen. At first we thought our parrot cage had fallen down (it was suspended from the ceiling near the stairs) but after checking both the kitchen and upstairs nothing could be found to account for the noise we had all heard. Life continued with things being moved or completely vanishing never to be seen again, until one night my husband woke to see a figure standing next to our bed. The ghost was a man about forty years old wearing pyjamas and a dressing gown. He seemed to be looking for something on my husband's bedside cabinet and was visible long enough for us notice a lot of detail. He had dark curly hair and the dressing gown was of a plaid material, the strange thing was my husband felt no fear and the ghost gently faded away.

We decided to ask some discreet enquiries as to who had lived in our house before us hoping this might shed some light on our "guest". Next door lived a very understanding old couple that had lived next door over fifty years. They didn't laugh when we mentioned our experiences. When we told them the description of the ghost, they realised it was Reg, a man who had lived in our house and died of cancer in his forties.

We still hear the odd band and things still move around the house but if we can't find something we just ask Reg to return it back to its original position. We are no longer frightened of our ghost and even our dogs who used to be very nervous of our bedroom, sleep fine now.

The old couple next door recently told us that our house has changed owners many times over the years, I can only think we are the only family that didn't mind sharing their home with a ghost.

THE OLD VICTORIAN HOUSE

My family and I have lived in our house for almost three years, a plaque at the very top of the house indicates that it was built well over a hundred years ago.

Since moving in, my mother and I have experienced many unsettling incidents. My own bedroom (in the attic) seems to be the setting for the majority of strange goings on. One night two years ago, I awoke as something heavy fell onto my bed, it felt like a football but when I summoned the courage to look at the end of my bed, there was nothing there.

On one very memorable occasion I felt my bed lift from the floor, about a couple of inches. I have been woken many a time by the sound of coat hangers being clashed together behind the curtains of my 'walk-in wardrobe'.

The most terrifying experience occurred when I had allowed our dog to sleep in my room, following a series of unsettling nights. I felt safe in his presence but I awoke for no apparent reason during the night to find my dog stood in the middle of my room staring right at me. I called his name but he continued to stare for the longest five seconds or so of my life.

At times, I can feel something with me in the room but cannot explain this sensation. My mother is a sceptical, matter-of-fact person, so when she told me of her experiences, I felt reassured that my experiences weren't the result of a vivid imagination.

My mum was once in my bedroom when she heard the distinctive sound of the huge front door opening and shutting. The house vibrates when the door is closed and my mum swears that she felt and heard this, she was convinced someone had come into the house. She called out twice, but no reply came. Quite afraid at this point, she crept downstairs - checking every room on her descent, certain that somebody was in the house. There was nobody but the cellar door was wide open - despite having been locked beforehand.

A similar thing happened last year, this time my mum heard someone or something enter through the front door. She was in her bedroom, which is situated directly, facing the top of the stairs from the downstairs hall, the front door itself is also directly facing the stairs. She heard the door open and close, then heard a female voice call out, "Mum!" She heard the voice clearly as it seemed so close. After a search again of the house, she found no explanation for the sounds she had heard.

The last experience I will mention is another from my mum. She awoke in the early hours of the morning and got up to make herself a drink. She sat in the living room as she waited for the kettle to boil, watching muted TV. She described to me a feeling coming over her, and sensed something behind her. The hairs on the back of her neck stood up and she froze in terror. This lasted for a few seconds before she felt free somehow to run out of the living room and upstairs to her bedroom.

I was the next person to go downstairs that morning, as I woke early to go to work. I was confused to find the living room door wide open. The light switched on as well as the TV. I brushed it aside and went to work. Only when I returned I was informed of my mum's ordeal and the urgency she had felt to leave the room.

EERIE WELSH MOUNTAIN HOME

I have always been able to see and sense the supernatural. My family have got used to it over the years and fortunately never made a huge fuss about it or tried to tell me I hadn't seen things.

I have lived in many old houses, our farmhouse was built around the sixteenth century and is haunted. Both myself and my grandmother have seen different things at different times.

When I married my poor long suffering husband also learned to put up with my 'feelings' about places. When buying our first house together I got him to agree that if I had a 'bad feeling' about a place we wouldn't buy it.

Anyway over the years I have seen and sensed so many things that I basically take it as normal, I am just one of those people who are tuned in, nothing special or clever, just on the right wave length.

Finally our dreams of moving to the Welsh Mountains came true five years ago. We moved over and rented an old house in a small town on the edge of the mountains. We had not seen the house prior to moving as it was only planned to be a stopgap until we found something to buy.

We moved in the same day as I first entered the house. Oh dear do I wish I had seen it before! The atmosphere was like walking into cold treacle, the house was dark, sad and felt really unhappy. The first week we heard noisy footsteps stamping up and down the stairs, because of this activity we did a little research into the house, as we weren't getting much sleep.

The house was very old and it had a chequered history. It had been a drovers inn, a Rectory (twice), a Gentleman's residence, a family home and over the last few years it had been rented out to tenants who had never lived there long. I began to feel the house was unloved, uncared for and really badly abused by the tenants - no wonder it wasn't happy with us, yet another set of tenants.

One night after about a fortnight of general noise it came to a head, the lights began to dim erratically so we went to bed and then that is when it all really kicked off. The thumping up and down the stairs sounded like a herd of elephants, the slamming of doors was getting worse and the atmosphere felt really bad. My husband and I had such a sense of fear and dread it was appalling. Finally it sounded as though a party was going on downstairs in what was originally the snug bar when it was an Inn.

I was by now more livid than frightened after having my sleep disturbed for the last fortnight by a ghost. I stood at the top of the stairs landing and bellowed at the top of my voice, "I have had enough of this, we are staying and we are living here, you can either stay and behave or **** off right now, its your choice!"

I stomped back to bed, in a foul mood, sat there, listened and waited and the whole house was silent. Finally and thankfully I got some sleep. The next morning with hubby off to work, I stood in the centre of the house, feeling like a complete idiot but also feeling I had to do something.

"Right you lot," I started. "We are staying, we live here too, if you live by the rules I am quite happy for you to stay, but if you misbehave I will do everything I can to get you out!"

Everything calmed down after that, the atmosphere changed dramatically and it became much happier so much so we bought the house six months later. Mad as it sounds we always tell the house what we are going to do when we do alterations i.e. new kitchen etc. The only time the "residents" as we call them are active is when new people come to stay for the first time. I think they like to check them out.

One particular time when my sister came over from Australia, my niece was asleep upstairs in the back bedroom and my hubby had gone up to bed early. This left my sister and I to settle down for a long chinwag in the snug. The door to the snug opens on to the hallway and from the armchair you can see the stairs. We had left the door open to listen out for my niece in case she woke up.

After a couple of hours chat I heard footsteps on the stairs, I glanced towards them but no one was there. My sister craned her neck from the opposite chair and said, "Emms must have got up I can hear her." "No she hasn't" I replied. "Yes," my sister insisted, "I just heard her coming downstairs." "Look for yourself" I told her, she did and of course the stairs were empty. Unconvinced she went up to check on my niece, who was sleeping soundly. I might add my husband was also still in bed and fast asleep.

We now love this house very much, it has a peaceful atmosphere and we are slowly making it a lovely family home. I generally don't tell visitors in advance about the residents, I just wait until breakfast the following morning for the usual questions about footsteps on the stairs.

TWO YEARS IN A HAUNTED FLAT

Seven years ago, my partner and I moved into a fairly modern housing association property. When we moved in, we investigated the loft to assess the space for storage, as the flat itself was very small. We found lots of odd nic nacs in the loft and things that you wouldn't really expect to find there but we did not think anything of it.

It was after disturbing the loft or possibly during decorating the lounge area things started to happen. Items would go missing just out of eyes view within seconds of putting them down. The spare room was not liked by visitors and we had complaints from my young nieces and nephews that they heard scratching in the room.

An adult friend was woken in the night by what she described as a series of flashes, not unlike a camera flash effect. This same room became the subject of many nightmares I myself endured almost every night. One night I woke from a dream in which I was frozen to the spot by an unseen entity. On opening my eyes I found myself in the same position with the same atmosphere around me, but cannot be sure that it wasn't just the effects of the dream. I was scared enough to stay very still and hold my bladder until morning.

The spare room door also did not like being closed. Initially, it had a thick plastic handle. However, this snapped in my hand sending me flying into the bathroom. We had it replaced, but again when attempting to shut the door, this came off clean in my hand, the screws intact and the holes in the door unaffected. We avoided the room and anything we had kept in there, remained boxed. In addition to these events, we heard banging noises around the flat as if something had fallen, but there was never anything there.

While off work sick one time, I heard my partner enter the property only they never entered the room. Two hours later they really returned. Our dog would constantly stand at the top of the stairs and bark at the wall. We found scratch marks on one of our board games, we had only played it once and it was put away immediately. These marks were similar to what we had found that were drawn around the entire walls of the spare room. These marks were not made at child height, but rather that of a teenager or adult.

I hated the property. The feeling, the complaints from guests. We did not get on well with the neighbours either and used their menacing of us as an excuse to transfer to another property. We did not think that saying the place was haunted would work so well!

Just before moving, my sister came to stay with us, awaiting a move of her own. We did not tell her of any of the events or other guest's complaints of the spare room. She stayed in the room for the first few nights with no trouble, then when my partner and I went out one night, my sister offered to watch the dog for us. We returned from the pub to find my sister sitting on the edge of the sofa clutching the dog. She told us that she had heard knocking on the lounge door and banging on the back of the kitchen shutters. She also laughed telling us that the dog had levitated off the sofa, dropping to the floor. She refused to carry on sleeping in the spare room and from then, resided in the lounge with my partner and myself.

As you may gather from the last sentence I have written, the room we refer to as the spare room should have been our bedroom. We resided in the property for two years and only ever slept in that bedroom for two nights, on the second of these nights, we both awoke during the early hours with disturbed thoughts and returned to the lounge.

The transfer date finally became a reality and we began to pack all of our belongings. The paranormal activities had calmed down at this point, making it almost bearable to continue living there. However, on the last night before our move would commence, we had removed several boxes from the loft and packed stuff in them. With so much stuff about such a small flat, these boxes were stacked just in the entrance to the lounge.

My partner went into a deep sleep and coldness began to enter the room. My sister and I tried to wake my partner, but it did not work. I knew immediately that the cold was coming either from the spare room or the boxes. Either way, I wanted the lounge door to be shut so after coaxing one another, my sister and I moved the boxes quickly into the hall and hurried back to our beds. The day of the move was tense. Having been given the keys to the next property, we only had a day to move all of our belongings. We could not afford a removal firm and so a friend helped us with her car instead. We got a good portion of items moved, but we were left with a lot more so the next day we handed in the old keys, but kept a pair so we could continue to move things. We had to hire a small van to move the sofa etc and had one person each end of the property move and one moving the stuff. However, this meant whoever was left at the old flat was alone.

On several occasions when we got down the stairs, we found the front door catch locked and top and bottom bolts across. This was really scary for us, but the door always opened without a problem. When it was my turn to watch the old house I sensed a tension. It was incredibly quiet and nothing was happening. I did not want to find out if anything would happen and so I sat on the doorstep with the door propped open. I reckoned if the door did shut behind me, maybe it was for the best!

In the two years we were at that flat, I had forgotten what a good sleep or a day without arguments was like. My partner and I have been in our present property for five years now. From time to time things move about or fall out of cupboards, but the atmosphere is not the same. I am not a psychic or anything, but from the contents of some of my dreams, I believe there were probably three 'energies' in the old flat. We still have one with us now - we think, but whatever was really bad could not come with us.

My partner and I don't argue anymore and I haven't had a single nightmare since the move. The one thing I do find to be strange is in the old flat we had many things go missing and had never found them. Since we have been in this property things still go missing, and we have also found things that don't belong to us. We seldom have visitors, yet we have found an extra toothbrush in the bathroom and a homemade band tape in my car. I have yet to listen to the tape, as it was a little unnerving finding it.

FINSBURY PARK GHOST

After my Auntie moved out of her house in 1988, I moved in to her house with my girlfriend, and our newborn baby. My Auntie had lived there for a while and it seemed a pleasant house to live in.

The house was a basement flat in Woodstock Road, Finsbury Park, although very old it felt very welcoming. After a week in the house we started to notice that directly above the toilet there was an airing cupboard, this door would constantly be open even though the catch worked perfectly well.

There was no breeze coming out or in but it would always be open. My girlfriend actually watched it open while in the bath once! Freaky but no problem, then we started to have keys go missing, money, purses, tools, stupid small things you put down and then they would be gone!

We asked her aunt (the previous occupier) about this and she said, "oh weird things happened in that place all the time, take no notice and you'll forget about it." We decided to ignore these silly things but one night my girlfriend and daughter were staying with her father for the weekend so I was alone. I was so scared that I borrowed one of my mum's dogs to keep me company for the night, an eight-year-old rottweiler called Ella. It was a big mistake, Ella spent the night nervously shaking by the back door and waking me throughout the night with loud barks. This was completely out of character for her although she was a soppy old thing, she had never acted like this before.

Anyway I told my mum and nan about this in the morning and they decided to come to the house to check it out. Nan was very spiritual and often 'picked up' on things. I'll never forget her standing in the kitchen of that place and in the time it took to boil a kettle she said, "I don't think you should stay here anymore and you're welcome to come home with me now!" I declined as my girlfriend was enroute home and I said that I'd keep it in mind.

Later my girls returned and we visited my mum's for dinner, she then drove us back to the house and my brother helped bring the babies buggy in and put it in the bedroom. In the bedroom we kept a jar of sweets so my brother and I helped ourselves to a handful each and he left. I shut the front door walked past the bedroom, all was well in the house and I joined the girls in the living room.

About half an hour later I went to put the baby in her crib and on entering the room I couldn't believe my eyes! The cupboard was open with clothes strewn everywhere, the bed was tipped up and the crib was on it's side. The room looked like someone had gone crazy in it and I immediately checked the windows for an intruder. I called my girlfriend in and she asked why I had done this, I explained what I had found and we just stood in silence.

I started clearing up and this feeling came over me as if someone was laughing at me, my girlfriend also felt the same. We put it out of our minds and got ready for bed, the baby was sound asleep and all felt calm. At 1:30am we both awoke to the sound of the baby cooing in her crib, I looked at her but she was looking past me and smiling at something. I couldn't workout what she was looking at but noticed the room was extremely cold. Suddenly the baby screamed as if she had been pinched or hurt, we grabbed our things and moved into my mum's house.

I returned the next day and the whole house was ransacked, the bed was upside down, cupboard tipped over, the contents of the kitchen cupboards thrown across the floor - you name it, it was everywhere. I spoke to the Aunt again after moving out and she said it had happened in the past but it would stop when you got used to it. I obviously thanked her for not mentioning this before we moved in.

A12 ROAD GHOST

Me and my wife were travelling North on the A12, driving back to Lowestoft from Ipswich. It was about 10:00pm on 9th August 2001. I was approaching the Beccles turn when a cyclist pulled out right in front of me from the junction.

I was travelling at sixty miles per hour and could not stop in time and the cyclist turned and smiled at me as I hit him.

There was a large impact.

Immediately after I stopped and I got out of the car. There were vehicles by this time slowing down behind me. I checked all round the car for the cyclist. I looked underneath the car, there was no sign of him. Not even any sign of the pushbike he was riding. I ran back to ask the people in the car behind me if they'd seen anything - they hadn't.

My wife phoned the police for them to check the area in case the cyclist was thrown to the side of the road somewhere. They found no sign. There was no damage to my car, even though I had felt a large impact. The police told me that this incident wasn't the first, and probably won't be the last.

They claimed that there is a ghost which haunts this stretch of the road. Fifteen years ago a young man in his late teens was cycling on the A12 and after the Beccles turn, the cyclist pulled out in front of a car too early and was killed. The ghost of the cyclist really gave me and my wife a fright on that August night. I have travelled up and down the A12 and passed this scene many times after this incident, but have not seen the ghost since.

MJ Wayland writes, as fantastic as this sighting sounds, the A12 cyclist has been witnessed many times but with different appearances (!) – Roadghosts.com reported these strange sightings, "In 1981 Andrew Cutajar encountered the figure of an old man on the A12 near Hopton, Norfolk, through whom he passed as he skidded out of control in his attempt to avoid a collision. On 15th July 1988, The Sun newspaper described police bafflement at the 'disappearance' of an elderly cyclist after being 'flattened' by a thirty-eight ton articulated truck driven by Frenchman Didier Chassagrande. The driver told of dragging the unconscious and bloody cyclist to the roadside before seeking help. He returned with police to the scene on the A12 at Kelvedon, Essex, shortly afterward, but all that could be found was the old man's torch, pump and his false teeth!"

A MEDIUM'S FRIGHT

MJ Wayland writes, Ian Doherty is one of Britain's most popular investigative mediums and aura artist, I am lucky to say that he's a good friend as well. I have taken part in private investigations with Ian and trust his word in what he's sensing and describing when he uses his mediumship skills. I asked him to write about a terrifying ghost encounter he once had while working for Fright Nights.

"I was working as the medium on a ghost hunt at the Galleries of Justice, Nottingham and was for the main part working in the cells area including the overnight and "hanging cells" of the buildings. After conducting some vigils in this area, I had sent my group for a well-deserved cuppa and had then gone down into the lower levels, notably the caves to inform my fellow colleague that I had sent my group for a break.

My guide said to me, "Ian there is no one down there." "I have to check," was my answer, and as such I proceeded through the underground chapel and into the cave area, and of course no one was there. I said sorry to my guides for not taking them at their word and turned around to make my way to the upper floors.

It was at this time when I heard a noise which to me sounded a like a person heavy breathing and growling at the same time. I have to say that I do not get scared at these events as I see ghosts and spirits every day of my life. What was different here however is that I was not expecting to be caught so off guard, in a dark cave within a building which is haunted and renowned for its poltergeist like activity. I turned around to face my aggressor to be faced with nothing.

"What did you do that for?" I asked.

There was then the very unnerving feeling of an energy rushing towards me, my hackles raised a little, for I could definitely feel "his" presence though not being able to see him. I backed away a little and asked, "why are you not showing me yourself?" Again a rushing sensation was felt and I shouted, "I am not going to run so why are you trying to scare me?" Again an overwhelming urge to run came over me, I dare say partly due to the increased adrenalin that was now pumping around my body, and the fact that I could still not see this man.

I turned around and began to walk back into the chapel area when again the rushing sensation was felt and this time very strong indeed. I turned around to once more be faced with nothing but the darkness of a corridor, lit only by a security sensor which cast shadows further down the corridor. I stopped, my mediumistic senses on full and again stated, "show me yourself!" This time the man showed himself to me. He was a tall figure of around 5 feet 9 inches tall, decked in a Victorian garb. His hair was dark in colour, cut quite short in length and his facial features were thin and drawn, his eyes seemed ever so dark and sunk back under a large brow.

"Why have you tried to frighten me," I asked again and was met by yet another wave of rushing and the urge to run, I wondered if he was laughing at me?

I told him to leave me alone and that I was not going to be frightened or intimidated by him. I turned and strongly resisted the urge to run, calmly as I could I walked through the chapel and to the stairs leading to the cells area – the rushing feeling once more made the urge to run almost overpowering! I continued to walk up the stairs resisting the urge to turn around and look back – it was not until I had walked past the cells area and through the large wooden doors that the feelings subsided."

Ian's reports about his ghost hunts and also examples of his Aura artistry can be found at http://www.aura-artz.co.uk/

OUR STRANGE HOLIDAY

We had a family Christmas holiday in 1993 in a very old farmhouse on the outskirts of Whitby. The surrounding area was very desolate and the farmhouse was split into two dwellings. The other half of the house had a family living there which we got the impression they were renting.

The farmhouse was very plain and wasn't really a pleasant place to have an holiday, especially in the winter as the heating was the storage type and it was very cold. We even complained to the owner (who didn't live there) as we felt it was not suitable for winter lets.

Anyway, I was sharing a very large bedroom with three of my cousins and the youngest was only around 18 months old. To stop him falling out of bed (due to the strange surroundings) we decided to put all three single beds together. The youngest was in the middle and me and my other cousin at either side in the other beds, but they were firmly pressed together. My other younger cousin was opposite on their own in another bed. In the corner of the room was a blocked up doorway which obviously led to the other farmhouse.

One night (unfortunately I cannot remember which) we had just gone to bed, shivering as normal. It wasn't long into the night when all of a sudden the bottom of the bed felt like it was lifted or knocked with some force. I wasn't asleep at the time and it obviously startled me so I called out to my cousin next but one, I said, "did you feel that?" She replied, "yes, but what was it, it felt like my bed was knocked?" After a lot of discussion we could not find any explanation. My other cousin opposite never woke up and the little one in between was fast asleep.

The next morning, obviously excited but at the same time scared we told all of the other family members, and tried to recreate it but couldn't move the beds with the same amount of force as the previous night. We always got the impression that because we changed the beds around, "someone" didn't realise the furniture had been moved and walked straight into the bed. However we couldn't recreate the force that the beds moved. We didn't experience anything else for the rest of the holiday.

After a few days had gone by and with our constant talking about our 'poltergeist', my grandad finally told us that he also had an experience a couple of nights before ours. One night during the holiday, he couldn't sleep as normal and in the middle of the night had gone down to the kitchen to fetch some water.

On entering the kitchen he could see a strange light in the courtyard, it seemed to be moving strangely but no matter how he tried to gain a better view, the patternation of the window obscured his vision. He ran to the lounge window and could quite clearly see a light hovering in the middle of the courtyard, it was not dissimilar to an oil lantern that miners would carry – except grandad could clearly see that no one was holding it. The spectral light moved to the right of grandad and he watched as it drifted out of sight.

We checked with the family next door who was renting the farmhouse and the husband was away for a few days and the lady was alone with her children, she certainly wasn't walking around in the middle of the night. I have always had an interest in the paranormal but never experienced anything first hand until this experience. We could not find any explanation as the beds were made of heavy wrought iron – so who or whatever moved our beds that night certainly had a lot of power behind them.

M62 ROAD GHOST

On Wednesday the 27th of November 2004 my husband was working nights as a truck driver on the M62 near Whitley Bridge. He was travelling along this stretch when he nearly knocked over a lady walking down the hard shoulder, she was dressed in a g-string and a jumper! Thinking it was someone who had possibly been attacked he pulled over fifty yards up the road from her and got out of the truck to help. She walked up to him and he asked her if she was ok?

She just muttered something turned around and started walking in the direction she had come from. My husband then got back into his truck and called 999.

The police came along with the helicopter with the heat-seeking camera (it was 11.30pm) but she had completely vanished. Because there had been no other reports to the police about her it seems like the only person who saw her was my husband (by the way his brother was with him and he saw her too).

What was she doing there at that time of night? Why didn't she accept help? And where did she go? Nothing adds up and we are coming to the conclusion that what they saw was a ghost!

MOSS VALLEY GHOST

Between the North East Derbyshire villages of Eckington and Ridgeway is an ancient wooded valley in which the River Moss runs. This area, now rich in wildlife, was once the centre of a metal industry, relics of which can still be seen today.

On August 24th 2002, two women, Cath and Carol took their dogs for a walk along the wooded paths of Moss Valley, a walk they undertake on a regular occurrence, but something would happen on that day to change their lives.

As they were walking along the path Cath noticed high in the trees what seemed to be a white carrier bag milling around. It began to float to the ground and at this point Carol noticed the bag.

Suddenly the "bag" began to enlarge and manifest into a very large white shape. As the shape became clearer, the women realised it seemed to be a woman on a large white horse - the apparition had to be near eight feet tall. As they stood staring at the "ghost", it swayed to and fro; then it glided round a bend in the path, disappearing from view.

Cath and Carol decided to go follow the apparition and see if it had continued down the path. When they reached the spot, they released not only was there no bend in the path but the apparition had disappeared. Suddenly around the women a horrible smell like rotten eggs could be smelt and as they walked along it seemed to follow them. Later the smell dispersed only to reappear in a different part of the woods. Interestingly, through all this experience the dogs were totally unaffected.

Over the last twenty years there have been anecdotal occurrences such as poltergeist activity as well as sightings of "shadows" in the woods but no white lady on a horse. The path that runs through Moss Valley was and is still highly pedestrianised. In the valley Roman remains have been found as well as 16th century artifacts. In the Victorian times the area would have been thick with industry in the week, but at the weekend it was a popular picnicking area. It's possible that the "ghost" could have been someone who regularly visited the area.

Since the sightings Cath and Carol have on numerous times had the horrid smell return and poltergeist activity but in different locations. Two weeks after the sighting, during walking across a field, they heard a large thud behind them. They turned and saw a large rock in the middle of the field, slightly damaging the grass. There was no one in the field with them, and they were standing in the middle! Sometime after that while walking through the woods again, one of the dogs lost his ball and he was becoming quite agitated about it. Cath shouted, "OK, give me back blue's ball" and out of nowhere the ball came out of the woods. As Cath and Carol pointed out, they take five dogs with them on each walk, if someone was in the woods; the dogs automatically walk up to them out of curiosity.

GRANTHAM ROAD GHOST

In 1972 I owned an MG midget which I used to drive to work in Grantham. I really enjoyed thrashing round the lanes in it, and got to know all the local byways. Several of the roads round Grantham have names: The Ramper, The High Dyke, The Four-wheel. I understand it's to do with the names of the stagecoaches or carrier's carts that used those routes in the 18th and 19th century.

Several locals told me that The Four-wheel was haunted, but it was the best route home and anyway I was twenty-two and didn't believe in that sort of nonsense. One night, on the way home from the local folk club, the road was foggy and progress was slow. I discovered that if I got out of the car and stood up, the fog only came up to my chest.

It was a weird, cold night. Standing there with fog up to my chest and a starry sky above me. I had no idea exactly where I was and could see only a few half-familiar farm buildings sailing this sea of fog. As I stood there I heard the weirdest sound, a sort of distant howl. From the trees above me a dozen rooks clattered into the air and headed away, and an owl rose from the fog and shot off in the opposite direction. Then silence for several minutes. After that I started to hear the slow, steady, beat of hooves. They came closer and closer, apparently coming along the road in the direction I had just driven.

They got louder and clearer, and just as I felt they were upon me they broke into a gallop and swept past me. The fog didn't stir, there was nothing to see, but the sound receded ahead of me. It's difficult to localise sounds in conditions like that, but I felt that though they turned the corner I knew it was somewhere ahead. Certainly more rooks scattered ahead of me, from somewhere near the road. I had been cold before, but now I was frozen to the marrow. I got into the car and started the engine, hoping to run the heater up, and sat there. A few minutes later I heard snuffling noises and turned the engine off. The car rocked and shifted as though a pack of animals were rubbing against it - like when you get stuck in a flock of sheep. Then the noises suddenly stopped and all was still. Bare in mind this was an open top car and I saw nothing alongside the vehicle. I was within inches of whatever was buffeting the car, and dared not reach out to touch it. That was enough for me.

I turned the car round and drove back up the hill to Grantham and booked into the George Hotel for the night. I've driven that road a thousand times since, with no phenomena at all. When I asked the elderly folk about the haunting they were less than forthcoming, I suppose because I'd been so dismissive before. One of them did say that it was supposed to be haunted by a headless horseman, or a carriage with a headless driver but that's standard stuff for haunted roads, and he didn't seem to know much about it at all.

DEMATERIALISING ALARM CLOCK

MJ Wayland writes, Christine wrote to me after reading about time anomalies that had happened in Liverpool, whether her story can be attributed to a time anomaly or just strange ghostly activity we will never know.

This happened in 1990, a long time ago now, but I have never forgotten it.

It was a Saturday night in May, and I was getting ready to go out with my then fiancé. I had a small, battery operated alarm clock, a cheap thing a few inches square in size, and I took it with me into the bathroom so I could keep my eye on the time. I then took it into the living room (it was the only clock I had) and put it on the table so I could watch the time whilst I put on my make-up.

I sat on the sofa and whilst applying my makeup I kept glancing at the TV and at the clock on the table. And then, one time as I glanced at the clock, I saw part of it, the top left-hand corner, had gone. It looked just as if someone had bitten off the corner.

I couldn't believe it and simply stared at the clock, which then disappeared before my eyes. In fact, it dissolved, like ice in hot water. I thought, "this cannot happen" and carried on applying my make-up, and glancing at the TV, and back at the clock - except there was no clock, the clock was gone.

I went out with my fiancé and returned home at about 2:00am I immediately started searching for the clock. I lived in a small, three room flat and nobody lived there but myself. I searched high and low, in every single nook and cranny, and when I had looked everywhere, I looked everywhere again.

At about 6:00am I went to bed and when I woke, I searched in the garden! This was despite the fact that I had put the clock on the table myself and hadn't moved it. No one had moved it; I was alone in the house and there was no one there to move it.

I moved out of that flat three years later and as I was packing everything into boxes and bags, I kept my eye open for the clock but I never found it. Even as I was unpacking things I still looked out for it just in case it had somehow been put into a box inadvertently. But it hadn't and I never saw it again.

And I have absolutely no explanation of what happened that night; I don't drink, don't take any kind of drugs and have no history of mental illness or hallucinations. I saw a solid object vanish into thin air before my very eyes. I will never forget it and I still can't believe it.

ST GWENDOLINES, TALGARTH

I wish to tell you of an experience that I had not too long ago.

My father was a vicar at St Gwendolines in the town of Talgarth near Brecon in Powys. About six years ago the boiler flue cracked and my father called a repairman.

My father was due to visit a parishioner in hospital, so I volunteered to take the keys and wait for the repairman, who was due to arrive early afternoon.

Taking the opportunity to do something not many people get to do, I climbed to the top of the belfry, to take in the scenery of the surrounding town.

On my way back down the spiral stone steps, a strange feeling surfaced within my mind. The closest I can describe it is as if I had remembered a dream that I had perhaps once had, in which I was being pursued down a flight of spiral stone steps by something (definitely not someone) of indescribably malevolent intent.

This made me panic instantly, and I raced down the remaining steps, slamming the belfry door behind me and firmly locking it. A little shaken, I went outside to await the repairman.

Looking back on this experience in the cold light of day, I wonder if this was just the fancy of a 'believer', or... something else? Taking into account that this isn't the first strange feeling that I have had in that section of the town, I'm inclined to believe the 'sixth sense' theory.

WRINSTEAD COURT FEELINGS

A few weeks ago myself and my partner visited Blue Bell hill, we experienced nothing there but it was on the way back that we had a traumatic supernatural experience.

We were riding back towards Faversham through Hollingbourne, and just past the Ringlestone Inn before Doddington. We stopped at some woodland, both being pagans we like walking through woodland, so we had a bit of an explore following the signposted footpath but it didn't lead anywhere.

We turned round and walked back and decided to follow the footpath on the other side of the road up a small incline past a large tree, this footpath also ended abruptly at a barbed wire fence.

We decided to have a sit and rest, however after a short while I began to realise that I was getting very tense. I had a feeling of being watched and of extreme hatred and anger, at first I tried to ignore it but it just got stronger and I told my partner of my discomfort.

She was feeling the same discomfort, and as we acknowledged the feelings, they intensified. It was a very strong feeling of being driven away, that we weren't wanted there. We left as quickly as we could, but I felt very weak, my partner commented how pale I had become.

I needed her help in manoeuvring the bike back on the road because I didn¹t have the strength on my own, which has never been a problem before. Even after we left the feelings of anger, hate, fear and sadness stayed with us for a while. I didn¹t want to go straight home I just wanted to ride around and try to shake the feelings, but I couldn't, and I also had the feeling of my partner being pulled off the bike.

I couldn't feel her holding on anymore and my torso had gone numb, I had to look down to make sure I could see her hands on my waist. I felt as if I was carrying an unseen and unwanted passenger.

Finally I decided to go home as it was the safest place I could find, (I have a protection spell on the house). I decided to lie down and collect my thoughts as I was so shaken by the experience. I discussed the events of the afternoon with my partner and found that we both had the same feelings and she had become concerned by my appearance and the effect it had on me. We have since tried to find out more information about the area but found nothing of any significance. For readers we visited a gravel track which leads up from Wrinstead Court near Doddington, below Wychling, Kent.

CHALLENGING THE DEVIL

I'd like to if I may, to tell you about one of my many experiences I've had.

I've singled this one out because it's the only one that really freaked me out. It was a couple of years ago now, I was 21 or 22 at the time and still living with my parents in Halfway, Sheffield.

What happened is quite bizarre I was walking back from my local pub (I wasn't drunk as I had work the next day) and the shortest route back was through Eckington cemetery. Walking with a couple of friends we got towards the top of the cemetery and I had an overwhelming urge to challenge something to "show" itself. For some reason I decided to challenge Lucifer himself.

After I came to my senses I realised around half an hour had passed and my mates had left. As nothing had "shown" itself I decided to go home, just a five minute walk and left it at that.

Nothing happened for the next few days, then around Wednesday or Thursday all that changed. I was asleep and suddenly felt the most unbelievable pressure placed upon my right shoulder and a voice whispered (but in a gruff voice is the only way I can describe it) "you don't want to see me" at this point I started to struggle and fight back and this is when I woke up dripping in sweat and shaking.

I was scared to go back to sleep that night and for the nights that followed nothing even remotely similar happened or has since.

I was wondering if anyone else has experienced anything like this or it could have been my subconscious telling me not to be stupid, either way it freaked me out.

MY GHOST IS CALLED FRED

Many years ago my wife and I were living in a rented flat in an otherwise empty house in Sandgate, Kent. One night as we were sleeping I awoke momentarily and saw a small ball of light come in a partially opened window. It went round the room and hovered by the bed and then squeezed through the keyhole and out into the hall. My initial reactions were that it was ball lightning or some kind of insect and then went off to sleep again.

Shortly after that we started noticing things were disappearing and reappearing elsewhere. We would also hear running water and splashing and find on investigation our bathroom sink full of soapy water. As my wife was reaching for bed one day she felt a hand squeeze hers from an angle that was impossible for me to have achieved. We often woke up together feeling that something was standing by the bed. My wife had a very frightening experience whilst going to the toilet. Someone started rattling the door knob and groaning. Having completed in record time what she was doing she came looking for me with murder in her heart only to find me outside with the neighbour, even stranger later in the kitchen some one whispered over my wife's shoulder 'sorry' and hugged her.

One night we moved the furniture round and then retired to bed, I was awoken in the middle of the night when something pulling my hair quite hard. As I had a skinhead haircut this was a surprise! I woke my wife and being a coward (afraid this is so) I asked her to cross the room and switch the light on, she did and it let go of my hair.

With the light on we could see at the other side of our room our pet mice were out on the table and their cage had been knocked over. Presumably the ghost had stumbled into them because of the new furniture layout.

We came to call the ghost Fred, I don't know why, and he used to make his presence felt every now and then. For some reason he used to steal Christmas cake slices. My wife would often shout aloud that he could stay if he didn't ever show himself to her.

Fred had his uses and was good at recovering lost or mislaid items. I had to produce my driving documents for the police and couldn't find them so I asked, "If you know where they are Fred leave them out". My wife and I returned from work to find them laid out on the kitchen worktop. One day as I was hanging a picture on a beam near the ceiling, the frame broke and a large sheet of glass fell out edge first towards my bare feet on the stepladder held by my wife. I thought I was going to lose my toes with the sharpness of the edges, but the glass stopped a few inches from my feet, hovered then smashed into the wall horizontally. My wife said she hoped Fred hadn't hurt himself and later that day a message was written on a mirror that said "F O.K." in some ghastly clear jelly.

A curiously modern turn of phrase especially when you consider that he had left a previous message in latin "Salutates gratis" i.e. visitors welcome. Once I thought we had burglars due to footsteps upstairs. I went and got the neighbour and his two husky sons. We searched every room but found nothing, yet when we were standing on the stairs discussing this we heard footsteps on the landing at eye level. We turned and all of us saw the carpet depressed by unseen feet as they walked from one room to another.

One particular occasion I was supposed to pick my wife up from college at a certain time, I kept clock watching and half an hour before I was due to set off my wife walked in the front door – extremely angry! She asked me why I had not picked her up, we then realised that every clock in the flat had been altered by an hour, even my wristwatch. I later discovered there had been a four car pile up at the college roughly the same time as I would have picked my wife up. Was Fred displaying precognition?

When we moved to a new house we invited Fred to come and every now and then he still does odd things but we don't feel he lives with us but only visits. We only live about three miles across a sea bay from "Fred's flat".

MY EXPERIENCES AS A SECURITY GUARD

While working as a security guard I have had the luck to visit some amazingly historic and unfortunately haunted properties. My first experience as a security guard happened at an old manor house that was the headquarters for a well-known company. During one shift I was responsible for opening up as well as bringing in a huge armful of milk cartons. I managed to open the door and heard the sounds of running footsteps and the unmistakable sound of someone falling down stairs. There is a certain rhythm to the slithering thump you get. I dropped the milk and raced to the stairs to see what had happened – I couldn't see anything or anyone, so I reported the incident in the guard's log and was eventually called into the manager's office. I thought I was due for a sacking but was surprised to see the Managing Director of the company who owned the building sat with my boss. The M.D. told me that she had seen the ghost of a child in the upstairs corridor while on her own in the building, she was glad that I reported what I had heard as she now knew that other people had witnessed the haunting.

The second experience occurred at an industrial estate near the ancient city of Canterbury, very close to the Pilgrim's Way and next to a ducking pond. Looking through the window one night I heard a rapping sound on the other side of the window but nothing was there. I rang my boss and told him what had happened he said he was not surprised as there had been a number of weird things happening at the location. He also told me that I had been moved to this location as many of security guards had strange experiences and refused to work alone on the site. After that night guards with dogs were always posted on site and each night rapping, laughter and footsteps on the tin roof were often reported. The dogs suffered the most often spending the whole night whimpering or cowering underneath the car.

I was posted to an archaeological dig near the M20 and Saltwood Castle, they had been excavating burial mounds and also discovered roman cremation urns. It was situated near the railway and two guards had to be onsite due to transport police stipulations.

During the patrols I would become nervous at a particular spot near the dig, I would often wait at the other side of the field until the other guard reached me. This was totally alien to me as I was happier to stand next to exposed graves than walk next to the dig. I watched with interest as the topsoil was removed from the field and the archaeologists began uncovering the remains of a building and found human remains – exactly where I felt uncomfortable. There were no other burials in the field except where I refused to walk. Strangely they found a complete human skeleton buried underneath massive boulders, the archaeologists told me that whoever this person was they didn't want him getting up. The likely cause was that when alive, the man buried was a murderer, so they buried him face down and placed the rocks on top.

I doubt these are the last of my experiences as a security guard, after my first experience I expected to be scared of visiting new places, its actually the opposite, I can't wait to see if I'll witness more ghostly activity.

ASTON LANE GHOST PLANE

In May 1994, Tony Ingle was staying at his caravan at Laneside, Hope on the Derbyshire Moors. On that sunny afternoon of Friday 5th May, Mr Ingle took his eight year old retriever, Ben for a walk and journeyed to nearby Aston Lane when he had a strange experience.

"It was between 4:40 and 5:00 in the afternoon when I saw a huge old aeroplane about 50ft above the moors, banking to the left. It was obviously in trouble," Tony told me.

"Could you tell me what happened next?" I enquired.

"I was so convinced it was going to crash that I ran hundred yards up the lane to a gateway, I lost site of the plane at this point. I expected to see the wreckage of the plane but there was nothing at all. I was struck by the silence of the area."

I asked Tony, "Was there anything unusual about your original sighting that suggested you have seen something strange?"

"Well, this is the strange thing, when I thought back I realised that although I had seen the propeller turning, the plane was completely silent. A week or so later a local researcher showed me some photos of World War II aeroplanes and I was able to point out that I had seen a Dakota."

"Was there any significance in witnessing a Dakota aircraft?"

"I didn't know at the time, but David (a local researcher) researched my sighting and told me that in July 1945 just fifty yards from my sighting a USAF Dakota crashed in heavy mist. All the seven crew died, it was a terrible tragedy."

I asked Tony, "What are your thoughts on what you have seen?"

"I don't believe in ghosts, I am not like that. I can't explain what I saw and I find it disturbing."

"Is there anything you'd like to add?"

"To be honest I am sick of the coverage that I've had. Since I contacted the Sheffield Journal the story has appeared in the Daily Sport and a few others, my phone has never stopped ringing with paranormal researchers, TV crews and newspapers. I am fed up with the whole thing."

I thanked Tony for his interview and told him that I would call him in a few years time. Unfortunately this was not to be since he would move house a year or so later.

The area is very well known for sightings of ghost planes. During the mid-1980's crash investigator Gerald Scarratt was up on a 2000ft (600m) shelf near 'James Thorn', showing a group of aircraft archaeologists the site where a US Superfortress crashed during a routine flight on 3rd November 1948. The visitors spotted a man in flying gear standing behind Mr Scarrett, and asked who he was. Scarrett turned round and there was no there.

It has been put forward that they could have seen Captain LP Tanner, the pilot of the Superfortress.

GHOST OF THE TOWER

My father is a retired psychiatric nurse and used to seeing all matters of strange behavior and quite adept at 'sussing out' peoples wind ups. He now undertakes agency work for care homes to keep him ticking over and as such comes into contact with some unexplained phenomena.

One night he was asked to report to an old care home which was converted from an old Victorian orphanage. He used to provide one to one consultancy with patients and was carrying out his duties as normal until his rest hour came up. During this time staff usually take a short nap and he was told there was a bed up in the tower.

The tower was a false turret that had been added to the building to make it more stately looking, however it still had a winding staircase and a room at the top for privacy. He went for his sleep but felt very restless and couldn't sleep because of all the noise of footsteps and voices coming from the staircase. He was used to members of the medical profession playing pranks so he laid there listening to them messing around on the stairs. He decided not to mention what he had heard as he thought people were having a laugh at the expense of the 'agency guy'.

Later that night an old lady took a turn for the worse and had to be moved to a private area so that she could be better treatment. She was taken on a wheeled bed into the lift accompanied by my father and another nurse. As they emerged from the lift he felt as he put it, "a pinch on the arse", thinking it was the other nurse getting fruity he gave her a funny look and pushed the bed down the corridor. The other nurse went to the front of the bed to guide it along and my father continued pushing from behind. He suddenly felt a push in the middle of his back, he looked round and no one was there. Then there was an almighty slap on the back of his head and what sounded like a child's giggle.

By now he was getting quite spooked and pushed the bed a lot quicker and placed the old woman into the area where she needed to be.

He finally decided to tell the other staff about what had been happening, and they weren't too surprised! They began to tell him about the ghost of a young boy who haunts the tower and that he shouldn't worry as all the playfulness means the boy likes him. Apparently the young boy died of one of the diseases that abounded in Victorian times and the tower was used for quarantine.

He's been back since, but doesn't stay in the tower anymore, he's had a few more playful pushes but he doesn't mind and seems to like the fact that a little kid from years ago can still have fun.

THE HAUNTED BED

My dad is a very rational man who for all his working life has never encountered 'ghosts' or experienced paranormal activity. In fact he worked as a security guard for a number of years often visiting stately homes, abandoned factories and crypts, yet he never felt that he was in the presence of ghosts or that he had an experience of some kind.

One day a family friend was going for a long weekend holiday and asked my dad if he could stay at his house since there had been vandalism and a group of lads hanging around outside. Dad agreed and over three nights was going to stay in his friend's house.

The house was once two shops with an upstairs maisonette type accommodation, and was built in the mid-1800s and purchased by the friend's family, the property had stayed in the family all this time. The family were very security conscious and had installed security lights all around the property. They asked if Dad could sleep in the unused side of the house, as they were planning on locking the other side – so if any sounds came from that side, Dad would know there was a burglary.

The first night came and went, Dad woke in the middle of the night and heard voices but put this down to passing punters returning from the pub.

The second night was equally uneventful, it was very peaceful and Dad was able to sleep all night.

On the third night, Dad told me that he felt a little strange sleeping in the bedroom he was allotted. He struggled to get to sleep and the room seemed colder than before. Soon he drifted off and in the middle of the night he awoke needing the toilet. He left the bedroom and walked down the long corridor, again he heard voices but thought it was people outside and none of the security lights were on. On the way back to the bedroom he thought he heard footsteps but again, being rational thought it was the settling of floorboards in the property. He climbed into bed and soon fell fast asleep.

He awoke early with the sunrise, there were no curtains to the windows but as he tried to get out of the bed he realised he was stuck! He lifted his head and could see that the bed sheets had been perfectly tucked in all around the bed – and so tightly that he struggled to get an arm free! Now Dad is very logical, and he lay there trying to workout how he could have climbed into bed and tucked himself in so tightly that he couldn't move. He told my mum and I about the experience which clearly had him vexed, he really couldn't work it out.

76

When the family friend returned later that day, Dad was straight down there to get an answer. Dad came back an hour later and he looked a little white. When asked about the bedroom and bed that Dad had slept in, he was told that the bedroom isn't used anymore because of its previous usage. The friend's mother and father had both died in that room and even in that very bed (individually). Not only that but the family used the room to position and prepare the corpse, as well as tucking them in the bed so that family and friends could pay respects before burial.

I think what freaked Dad out the most was maybe the 'ghost' mistook him for a corpse and had tucked him in. I am sure he thought it was an omen or sign for a while, but I can confirm ten years later, Dad is still around and rational and dismissive of the paranormal as always. Although if you ask him about that night he quickly moves the subject on but on rare occasions he will admit he couldn't explain what happened to him.

MORE FROM THE AUTHOR

I hope you enjoyed my first collection of original ghost experiences and the vast array of phenomena reported by the witnesses. If you would like to submit an experience or was a witness to some of the stories in this book please email mj@mjwayland.com

For further ghost stories and research as well as my future releases please visit my website - http://www.mjwayland.com/

Thank you

MJ Wayland

My other books include:

50 Real Ghost Stories
Real Christmas Ghost Stories
The York Ghost Walk
The Derby Ghost Walk
Tales of the Polden Hills
The Northern Tradition

CPSIA information can be obtained at www.ICGtesting.com
Printed in the USA
LVOW13s1728040814

397434LV00003B/647/P